Amazon Echo
The 2016 User Guide And Manual
Get The Best Out Of Amazon Echo
By Martin Butler

Table of Contents

Foreword

It's dinner time in the Butler household and an argument has unfurled its ugly wings. A trivial question at which many you will probably smirk. Is Great Britain the same as the United Kingdom? My eldest believed them to be the same and my younger daughter claimed that Northern Island was the difference. As a seasoned user of the Amazon Echo now, this argument would have never even occurred. However, at this time it was a brand new addition to the home and it took me a while to think of calling upon its impressive abilities.

"Alexa, what is Great Britain?"

"Great Britain is the official name given to the island upon which England, Scotland and Wales sit."

Silence at one end of the table, hysterical laughter at the other end. Argument over, problem solved.

As a fervent user of Amazon Echo for almost a year now I have learned a lot about the device and Alexa. This user guide is designed to take you right through the basics from set-up to synchronization to your first interaction. Then I will take you through all of the cool and exciting things that Echo is capable of. Updated just in time for 2016, this guide is as fresh as it gets.

Read on, you're in good hands!

Introduction – The Personal Assistant That Dreams Are Made Of!

Amazon. Online behemoth, retail game-changer, impressive innovator and yet often negatively portrayed by the media. Whether you are a fan of Amazon or not, this invention, four years in the making is potentially their greatest yet. Hailing from the famous Lab126 offices, Cupertino, California. This subsidiary of Amazon is responsible for Amazon's Kindle devices as well as the Fire TV, tablets and phones. Amazon Echo is created by a team with a proven track record and a strong history of delivering products ahead of their time.

Codenamed "Project D" during the early phases of development, Amazon Echo was actually the first attempt to grow Amazon's portfolio of internally developed gadgets after the original Kindle. The Fire range of products made it to market first, but all the while the team were optimizing and perfecting Echo and Alexa (Who or what exactly is Alexa?! In a nutshell, your new best friend and you'll find out exactly why throughout the book!). Released fully to the world in June 2015 after a successful limited launch at the end of 2014, Amazon Echo is fast becoming a must-have home accessory.

So what does Amazon Echo do? The most commonly asked question when first encountering the device is difficult to answer briefly. Why? Because it is capable of performing such a wide range of tasks that explaining all of them would require a book length user guide (pro-tip: you're reading it!). Fancy hearing your favorite audiobook in the soothing voice of Alexa? Amazon Echo has you covered. Need to arrange day-to-day tasks such as shopping lists, cooking timers and alarms? You bet, you're covered. Finding out what the weather conditions are like before you have even opened your eyes in the morning, a further possibility. Having barely scratched the surface, you'll be glad to know that there are plenty of chapters in this book dedicated to helping you get the most from your device. Did I forget to mention that Alexa is one of the greatest settlers of arguments at the dinner table? Simply ask her to read any of Wikipedia's five million articles and witness one side of the table grow very quiet.

Okay, so Alexa? In essence, Alexa is Amazon's answer to Apple's Siri, Microsoft's Cortana and of course, Google Now. Alexa is the soul of the Echo, the beating heart and soothing voice that make the device so enjoyable to use. Collectively known as Intelligent Personal Assistants (IPAs) and joined in the market by many more than the aforementioned four, they are an early foray into the future envisioned by so many of us. Differing from common computing devices by their, at times, surprising ability to sound and feel human. It is quite easy to believe that you are speaking to a real person when engaging with IPAs. Reasoning, comprehending, learning and planning – all qualities traditionally reserved for living beings are standard practice for many of these software. It is very important to understand that whilst Alexa is already a useful tool, it is still in its infancy. Having received many updates in just the few months it has been available for, each introducing new and improved features, you can be sure that the developers over at Lab126 are working tirelessly to innovate, expand and fine-tune their baby's abilities. Amazon Echo and Alexa are here for the long-run, to be a staple in your home for the many years to come.

What makes Alexa stand out from the other IPAs? Aside from being an aesthetic, attractive device, Alexa comes with a myriad of features that places her leaps and bounds ahead of her competitors. Upon first use it becomes clear that Alexa's voice sounds natural and more human-like. The response time is market leading, allowing for quick results and enjoyable conversations. Do you live in a busy household with lots of background noise? No problem. Amazon Echo's microphones are exceptionally sensitive allowing for easy voice recognition and comprehension. Unlike many of the IPAs that are limited to smart phones and tablets, Echo can be connected to the lighting in your house. Allowing for voice controlled ambience control, and that is just the beginning of home integration planned for this device.

Now that I have introduced you to the product, let me take this opportunity to thank you for choosing to use this user guide. I truly hope I can help you get the same level of enjoyment from the device that me and my family have. Before diving into the potential uses, let's have a good look at the hardware, as well as a further look at why the Amazon Echo is the go to device in this field.

Why Choose Amazon Echo?

Since release, Amazon Echo has received a ton of attention from the media. Bringing in countless positive reviews since its first day on the market. As product improvements occur the reviews keep getting better and better. Receiving huge endorsements from publications as prolific as USA Today and CNET, Amazon Echo has created a huge fan base and for good reason.

"The Echo may be the closest thing we'll have to a Star Trek computer at home."
-CNET

"Echo could hear my voice even when music was playing loudly"
-USA Today

"With Amazon Echo it was love at first sight"
-Re/code

So what about the device is responsible for all this praise? Let's take a detailed look.

Ease of use

Amazon Echo has been designed exceptionally well and this is most obvious when considering how easy it is to set-up and use the device. Although touched upon later in this guide, the set-up instructions are clear and concise and make your first moments with Alexa very pleasant. I'm sure I'm not the only one who has been so excited to receive some new hardware, only to spend the next three hours figuring out how to turn it on! Not an issue with Alexa, even if you are very inexperienced with technology you will find the simplicity of the device a delight. In the very unlikely case that you are truly stuck, Amazon's famously good customer service is just a phone call away. Initial set-up quite simply consists of choosing a few personal preferences and settings and then you are good to go. Alexa's helpful nature will take of any questions or queries you have after this point.

Market-leading voice recognition

One thing that guests of my house are consistently surprised by, is that Alexa knows who it is having a conversation with. It can be very strange having your voice recognized and identified by software. This is still relatively new to the world and is not commonly used. I have to admit, it does become very endearing. Alexa effectively practices listening to your voice and gets better at understanding you over time.

Voice and sound quality

One of the distinguishing features of Amazon Echo is Alexa's voice. Friendlier and more life-like it is quite easy to believe you are having a conversation with another person when speaking to Alexa. Matching the voice quality is the general quality of sound when asking Alexa to play some of your favorite music. Whether you are in the mood to relax to some soft indie rock, or oppositely, dance to the latest and greatest house release, Alexa will impress.

Consistent upgrades and improvements

As you will picked up from the introduction, whilst complete and ready to use, Alexa is not yet a finished product. In fact, it is unlikely to ever be a finished product! The possibilities attached to this product are virtually limitless. Already you can control the lights, fans and some basic electrical systems in your house using Alexa. As the rest of your house catches up and furniture and appliances begin to integrate you will eventually be able to control your entire house with just a few words.

To give you a taster of how quickly the development team are rolling out new features take a look at what has happened just this year. Since the beginning of 2015 there has been a total of six official updates. The first two of these were general bug fixes, which is re-assuring as we can be sure that if any issues or bugs arise in the future the developers will be quick to fix it.

Version 2249 – Jan 28th - In this update Amazon added many additional voice commands related to the shopping list and to-do list features. This allowed the user to go back and review their lists and make editions.

Version 2332 – Feb 26th – Another important round of efficiency improvements, bug fixes and performance enhancements.

Version 2392 – Mar 30th – In this update Amazon added support for Belkin and Philips connected home devices.

Version 2530 – Jun 1st – A huge update that allowed users to listen to any of the audiobooks available through Amazon's audiobook company, Audible. There are currently over 150,000 audiobooks available through Audible. This is a very special update as it allows the user to listen to any audiobook through a voice they are familiar with.

On top of the official updates that have been released so far, Amazon consistently send out smaller updates that don't require new software. For example, in April Alexa received the ability to give live sports scores without updating the version of software running on the device.

These updates are just the beginning of a long and exciting list that is destined to fill this page in a few years' time.

Privacy

Due to the nature of devices of this kind, one of the major off-putting factors for many people is a lack of privacy. In order for Alexa to be able to respond when spoken too, she must be listening all day, every day. We know that Alexa has very responsive microphones and is able to pick up all the details of the sounds and conversations that surround it each day. Fortunately Alexa can ONLY record sound when it is in use. When you are not speaking to her she is only listening for the wake word and nothing more. To repeat and clarify, Alexa does not make recordings of sound when idle.

If you believe that your device has recorded a conversation or sound that you would like to delete. You simply head to the 'Manage my device" tab in the user profile, where you delete previous recordings.

Let's Get Physical – What To Expect When You Open The Box

If at any point you have purchased one of Amazon's Fire products, you may find yourself familiar with the aesthetic of the box that Amazon Echo comes in. The packaging is well made and space-efficient with a fiery orange interior. You will find five individual items in the box. The Echo device (10 points if you managed to guess that one!) and a voice capable remote control unit that handily comes with batteries. The remote control also comes with a magnetic holder. You will also find an AC power cord. Each of these items comes individually wrapped in protective plastic. Also in the box is the official set-up guide by Amazon, which contains many commands and questions that you can ask Alexa.

Important note: The remote is an additional extra, but comes very highly recommended as it provides you with the option to use Alexa even when you are out of range of the main device. Not only that, but it also allows you do basic tasks like volume control from a distance. If you have not ordered the remote as an extra, then of course you will just receive the Echo device, the AC power cord and the official set-up guide.

Weighing in at a fraction over one kilogram, the Amazon Echo device stands at just over 9 inches, 9.25 to be precise and has a diameter of 3.25 inches. Upon first touching the device many users are surprised by the unexpected weight. Primarily coming from the multitude of built-in speakers and amplification system. The crystal clear sound is produced by a 2.5 inch woofer (middle in the below picture) and a 2 inch tweeter (bottom of the below picture). The reflex port which can be seen inside the top of the device works as an amplifier and enhances the sound of the speakers for extra volume without distortion.

Image from techlicious.com

You may have cottoned onto the fact that Echo runs on AC power, being one of the few drawbacks to the device. Being the intelligent female that she is, Alexa requires some real fuel and should be plugged in at all times. The device quite simply does not have a battery.

The top of the device, pictured below, presents the "mute microphone" button, as well as the action button. Due to the nature of the device, unless you purposefully press the mute microphone button, it will be listening for your voice 24/7. Don't be put off by this fact though, as when you are not interacting with the device it is only listening for its wake word, Alexa. The action button can be used to interact with Alexa manually, as well as being key in the set-up process explained later on. The top half inch of the device can be rotated to either increase or decrease the volume. Also shown is the light blue ring of light that only emits light when you are interacting with Alexa. The blue ring is also where the seven microphones that give Alexa her impressive listening abilities. They are spaced out evenly around the ring with one right in the middle and use beam-forming technology to pick up sound from any direction whilst cancelling out background noise at the same time. You can see this in action when you speak to Alexa as the side that you are speaking to will light up! The image also provides plenty of ideas for using Alexa!

Image from amazon.com

Moving down the device towards the bottom you will notice, when plugged in, a small light that shows whether Alexa is connected to your Wi-Fi or not. When connected, the light will be white and when disconnected the light will be orange.

The remote control

If you opted to include the optional remote control, I'm sure you'll be wanting to know how it works! Unlike the Echo device which is primarily controlled by voice the controller can easily be controlled by either voice or by touch. Those familiar with the Amazon Fire TV remote control will notice similarities in appearance. The remote is roughly 5 inches long with an easy to hold rubber grip.

Happen to be on the far side of the room to Alexa and don't fancy raising your voice to get a request in? The remote has got your back, simply press the button at the top of the remote to activate the microphone mode.

So, onto those touch controls I mentioned. The Amazon Echo remote features a directional track pad that will allow you to quickly and efficiently control audio playback on your Amazon Echo. To be more specific you can pause and play, skip forward or backwards and control the volume using the track pad.

Quick tip: You do not need to say the wake word when you are using the remote, simply press and hold the talk button.

Let There Be Life - How To Get Started With Your Amazon Echo

Before we start: Make sure you have the Amazon Echo app installed on either your smart phone or tablet! The app works with Android phones and tablets running Android 4.0 or above, iOS phones and tablets running iOS 7.0 or above as well as Amazon Fire phones and tablets running Fire OS 2.0 or above.

As alluded to in earlier chapters, setting up Amazon Echo is remarkably simple. Get it plugged in and immediately it will begin to act as an internet access point via Wi-Fi. With the brief use of a smart phone or tablet to make a connection between Echo and your Wi-Fi.

As soon as Alexa detects your connection it will begin to direct you through the Echo app. The instructions are very straightforward and will enable you to complete this part of the set-up hitch free. A few things you will need to do during this process is to let Alexa know which router or internet connection to use in the house. You will also need to supply the password to your Wi-Fi.

Once this step is completed you will be prompted to watch a helpful orientation video which I genuinely recommend you check out. You can never have too much information about a device like this! The video covers a number of the basic voice commands and will leave you with a basic confidence on using the device.

Want the set-up in fifteen words?
1. Download the Echo app
2. Plug the Echo in
3. Follow the apps instructions
4. Job well done!

Okay so basic set-up has been completed but there is still plenty to do in order to optimize your experience with Alexa. Now that she has access to your Wi-Fi network it will take a maximum of five minutes for her to be ready to perform. This brief wait is due to the device checking for automatic software upgrades and in some cases installing them.

At this point you should be able to start speaking to Alexa and receiving responses. This is one of the most exciting times you will have with Alexa, your first conversation, so prepare something friendly to say! Experiencing her voice for the first time is a very interesting, as you will be getting hearing a lot of and getting used to this voice for the foreseeable future. Whilst I and many others are fans of the current voice, there is demand for alternatives, particularly male voices. Whilst this update is not in the immediate pipeline, it will undoubtedly happen at some point.

Wake words

In order to activate Alexa you must say the wake word. By default the wake word is Alexa. As soon as you say this word, your device will immediately come to life, shown by the blue ring of light on top of the Echo lighting up. This is the cue to let you know that Alexa has picked up your voice and is awaiting direction!

Of course in some homes, Alexa might not be a suitable wake word. For example you may have a family member that goes by Alexa, which could lead to a lot of confusion. In this case you have one alternative – "Amazon". Yes, admittedly this is a fairly limited choice but just like the voice, this is something that will definitely be expanded upon in the future. In order to change your wake word to Amazon jump onto the Echo app. Go to settings and then go to your Amazon Echo. Finally select Wake Word to make the change.

Now you are good to start using Alexa following the advice contained in subsequent chapters. I don't need to tell you again how impressive Alexa's voice recognition is, however there is something you can do to make it even better. Particularly now at the beginning of your relationship. In the Echo app you will find Voice Training. Whilst Alexa is impressively adaptive and the voice recognition software is a quick learner, it is possible to speed the process up and make life a little easier for both yourself and Alexa. This little 'game' takes no longer than half an hour and will train Alexa to recognize your voice much better. As she begins to learn your speed patterns she will be able to give more accurate, faster responses.

Before you begin the voice training, be sure to double check that your Echo is plugged in and that you are not using the remote control at all. The app will prompt you to say 25 different phrases. It can be tempting to stand right next to the Echo whilst performing this training but for the best results you want to be sitting or standing where you will often speak to Alexa. There is no need to speak slowly and no need to try and speak extra clearly. The whole point of this exercise after all is to help

Alexa adapt to YOUR personal voice and style of speaking. Treat Alexa like a friend!

Now, 25 phrases is quite a lot and I have to admit I made a couple of mistakes when doing my voice training. Fortunately the app has a pause button, and once this has been pressed you will have the option to "Repeat Phrase". When you have made it through the 25 phrases simply tap the "End Session" button. Alexa will the save your progress and update her system to better recognize your voice, especially when you say phrases contained in the test.

Before you read onwards: Every command, question or request you give to Alexa must begin with the wake word. You don't need to pause between the wake word and the rest of what you have to say, simply tagging "Alexa", or "Amazon" to the start of your sentence will work. Provided the device is plugged in, Alexa is always listening out for its wake word and will respond immediately every time. If you can recall from the previous chapter, there is a mute microphone button on the topic of the Echo. You can use this button to turn off Alexa's continuous listening, preventing response even when using the wake word. Fortunately you can continue to give voice commands through the remote controller when the mute microphone mode is on.

The second you say "Alexa" the blue light ring on the top of the device will light up and your Echo is now in action. After detecting the wake word your devices light will turn blue whilst it processes what you have said. If for example you asked to set an alarm and wasn't convinced that Alexa had got the message you could simply check the app for the latest input. Another little trick you can employ to be certain that Alexa is getting your message is to turn on the 'wake up' and 'end of request' sounds. To do this simply go to 'Settings' on the app and tap on 'Your Echo'. Finally, tap on 'Sound Settings' and enable either the wake up sound or the end of request sounds, or of course both if you like! Now every time you say the wake word and Alexa picks it up, the device will make a small sound. If the end of request sound is turned on, Alexa will make a small sound when it believes you have finished your message.

Dialog History

As you know, Alexa will record and save all of your conversations. Not to be misunderstood, Alexa will ONLY record when you are engaged in conversation with her, having used the wake word. Every conversation with you that Alexa records, is then stored in her memory and analyzed in order to improve future interactions. As well as storing the audio recording Alexa also creates a transcript of the conversation. This storage of conversations is called the dialog history and you may be glad to know that users can access and edit this at any time.

In order to find your dialog history jump onto your Echo app and open the settings tab. Once there tap the "Dialog History" button. Once this new window has opened you will be able to see all of your previous interactions with Alexa recorded in a large list. If you want to listen to one of the recordings, tap it and then click the play button. The recording should start playing immediately.

How can I delete a recording? There are a couple of easy ways to delete the recordings from your dialog history. You will need to decide whether you want to delete the recording from just the device or from both the device and the Amazon Cloud. If you want to completely delete one or all of your recordings tap on the culprit and the tap the delete button that subsequently pops up. Your recording has had all trace removed from both the device and the Amazon Cloud. If you just want to delete the Home Screen Card aspect of the recording to clear up your app's homepage then head back to the homepage and click on the remove button next to the recording you would like to delete. This method allows Alexa to keep the data from the conversation in the cloud to learn and improve from, whilst also allowing you to control and clean up your homepage.

Another option is to just eradicate all of the recording in your dialog history in one go. If this is what you want to do then head to your "Settings" page on the Echo app and tap the "Manage your Content and Devices" button. Select your Amazon Echo from the selection of devices that may show up on this page and then tap the "Device Actions" button. This will create a dropdown menu, on which you will be looking for "Manage Voice Recordings". Here you will find the option to "Delete all the Conversations". Be careful before deciding to use this feature as you will be completely wiping your Echo's memory. Every single recording it has made since you first started using it will be erased from the storage of the device as well as the Amazon Cloud. This should only be done after careful consideration, as the whole purpose of the recorded conversations is to enable Alexa to learn and improve its abilities. If you are concerned about privacy, rest assured Alexa is not to be worried about.

Bluetooth

A strangely overlooked feature is Amazon Echo's ability to connect with many other devices via Bluetooth. We know that through the app, your Echo is given access to music streaming services such as Spotify, iTunes and Amazon Prime Music. However if you are in the mood for a playlist, or perhaps just a song from your phone, tablet or otherwise Bluetooth enable device then Alexa can handle that for you. It is after all, in its very essence a speaker! All that is required to have your favorite tunes blasting out from Echo's quality speaker set up is a quick synchronization between the two devices.

Ensure your device's Bluetooth is switched on and searching, place it near the Echo. Now all you need to do is tell the Echo to pair with the device. "Alexa/Amazon, pair". As soon as the Echo has received this request it should say "Ready to pair". At this point you should notice your other device has picked up the Echo in its search. Quickly select the pair up option and upon successfully linking, Alexa will tell you "Connected with Bluetooth". Mission accomplished! You are now free to play all the songs on your device to your hearts content through the crisp bass and smooth sound of Alexa. When you are finished listening to your music don't forget to say "Alexa/Amazon, disconnect". This will turn of Echo's Bluetooth function and disconnect your secondary device. Just so that you are aware, it is only possible to play music from your device. It isn't yet possible to play the audio from a video for example.

After the initial set up with a device Alexa will remember it for any future repeats. All you would need to do is turn the Bluetooth of your phone or tablet on and connect to Alexa. This is a great perk for when you are relaxing after a tough day and would like to effortlessly put some calming music on.

A very cool and rare feature of Alexa is that when your device is connected to the Echo you can actually control the music hands free. Even though it is playing from your phone or tablet. In most cases when playing music via Bluetooth you need to control the music via the original device. Impressively, Alexa does it for you. Once you have synced the devices and started the music you can use the following voice commands to control the flow! Restart – Next – Previous – Stop – Play – Pause. Named the Hands-Free Voice Control for Paired Devices by the creators. This feature is a real blessing if you are like me and prefer to blast some music whilst doing the house work. Being able to move between songs whilst mid-scrub never gets old!

There are a couple of notable devices that are not yet compatible; Mac OS X devices in particular. It is expected that future updates will change this.

Connecting other devices to Amazon Echo

After completing the prior set-up of the device you may be keen to get your other devices such as SmartThings or Wink Hub connected to the Echo. Simply follow the instructions provided in the bullet points below to do this.

- Open up your Amazon Echo app.
- Press on the Settings button.
- Find and tap the Devices Links menu.
- Tap on Link With ...
- Find the name of the service that you would like to link your Echo with.
- Once selected, a log-in page for that service will appear.
- Simply input the relevant details and continue to follow the specific instructions for your service on the screen.
- Stage one completed.

Before you follow the above instructions make sure you have gone onto the manufacturer's app, for the device you are trying to connect to, and enable connection to Amazon Echo.

Now, to connect the actual device to Amazon echo you have two options. You can either tell Alexa to connect with the following command, "Alexa, discover my devices". The other option is to use the Echo app. Head to Settings and then tap on Connected Home Devices. Once on this page click on Add New Devices.

Alexa will then search for the device and upon successful connection will say "Discovery is complete. In total, you have 'number' reachable home devices under this Echo." If there is an issue she will say "Discovery is complete. I couldn't find any devices." You can also tell that connection has been unsuccessful by checking the app. It will appear as Unreachable. If this happens you may have to look at relocating one of the devices in order to make connection a bit easier.

Now that you have successfully connected the devices you are free to being controlling features of your house with your voice! If you want to connect multiple devices around your house to

Alexa, and be able to use them all at the same time you will need to create a group. Head into your Echo app and go to Settings. Click on Connected Devices, go to Settings and you be able to set up a group. Have fun switching things on and off with your voice! It never gets old.

The Amazon Echo App

As a truly essential part of the package, the Echo app deserves to be explained. It is the only way, outside of voice control and the remote to interact with the Echo device. Inside the app you'll be able to find the to-do and shopping lists you may have created through conversation with Alexa. You will be able to view the alarm functions as well as any timers you may have running. It can also be used to interact with the online music services your Echo may be linked to. Talking of music, the app can also act as a media player that can control the volume of the device.

When looking for inspiration the app can be a great source of ideas to use your Amazon Echo in new, unthought-of ways. It is frequently updated and refreshed with great information.

Much like the aesthetic of the Echo itself, Amazon have kept the app very minimalistic and simple to use. There is very little to see on the home screen, you will be able to see the recent commands you have given to Alexa as well as the recent questions you may have asked her. You will have the option to browse for similar content that is already on the app and offered links to find more information about the topic.

The top left corner of the screen is where it gets interesting. You'll see a small tab that when used will show all of the options available for your Echo. Four key things that you can currently view in the app are your to-do list, shopping list, alarms and timers. As well as them you are also able to see your music. Presently, Amazon supports music from iHeartRadio, iTunes, Pandora, Spotify, TuneIn and of course Amazon's own music service – Amazon Prime which happens to be the default setting. You can change it to any of the other services mentioned above in your app settings. A cool thing that I recommend doing is creating your own playlists. Especially handy when friends are coming around!

If Knowledge Is Power Then Alexa Rules The World

One of the main reasons that people, myself included, purchase Amazon Echo is for the easy access to knowledge that it provides. There has been no shortage of times in my life when I have been relaxing at home and a sudden thought or question has popped into my mind. Previously I would have to make the effort to get up, wait for my PC to load up just to ask a simple question. As you can probably guess, most of the time the question remained firmly in my head, to be forgotten soon after. Whilst yes, the recent advances of smart phones and tablets goes some way to solve this problem, Alexa takes it much further. "Alexa, who is the lead singer of The Cure?" Five seconds later you have your answer, done, simple as that. Not only does Alexa provide you with all the information you might require but she will update your app to show the information and further links. With the full force of Google and Wikipedia behind her, you will be hard pressed to stump Alexa.

Alexa would love to tell you about the local weather forecast for the current day, or for any point over the next week. You can also ask her about the weather in specific cities all over the world. As always, don't forget to tag the wake word to the beginning of your sentence. "Alexa, what's the weather like today?" Two seconds later. "Right now, in Philadelphia it's 83 degrees with clear skies and sun. The forecast for the rest of the day is mostly sunny, with a high of 87 and low of 75." Simply adjust the command to a specific place or time if that is what you require.

Amongst a whole string of other capabilities Alexa is great at providing word definitions or alternatives, sports news and even live sports scores. Geographical questions like capital cities and borders are fair game. Forgotten a local holiday date? Not to worry, Alexa never forgets and will always be there to help you. As a fervent baker, my wife will tell you one of the greatest features is Alexa's ability to make unit conversions.

"Alexa, how many grams are in seven ounces?" For example. For those of you who like me make a long commute to work each day, a helpful feature will be Alexa's up to date traffic reports. Allowing for alternative directions to be taken before encountering any delays!

As mentioned above, Alexa has full access to Wikipedia's five million articles. You can probably imagine just how much information this leaves at your fingertips. In order to get Alexa to begin reading a Wikipedia article you simple provide the command "Alexa, Wikipedia, Duncan Bannatyne". You need to say it in that specific format in order to get Alexa to read an article. "Alexa, who is Duncan Bannatyne?" Will give you a worth answer but will not give you the option to hear the full article about the man. Once Alexa has read the first paragraph of a Wikipedia page she will stop reading. At this point you have the option to hear more of the article by simply saying "More", "Hear more" or "Tell me more". Don't forget that you will find the link to the article in your Echo app shortly after asking the question.

Give me some more examples of what I can ask!

In the following pages I am going to give you a ton of examples that you can use to base questions and queries off. You may be surprised by the countless option on offer here! I certainly was when I began experimenting with Alexa. Simply take my prompts and adapt them to your own needs.

People

"Alexa, who is Jack Daniels?"

"Alexa, who is the President?"

"Alexa, who is the owner of the Dallas Mavericks?"

"Alexa, who plays drums for the Foo Fighters?"

"Alexa, who starred in the movie I-Robot?"

"Alexa, who was the president in 1965?"

Time, dates and holidays

"Alexa, what day of the week is Thanksgiving on this year?"

"Alexa what is the time?"

"Alexa, what is the time in New York?"

"Alexa, what is the time in England right now?"

"Alexa, when is Eid?"

"Alexa, when did World War Two finish?"

"Alexa, when did America become independent?"

Music and Movies

"Alexa, who sings the song California Dreaming?"

"Alexa, what songs does Miley Cyrus sing?"

"Alexa, who is the lead singer of Muse?"

"Alexa, in what year did The National release the album Boxer?"

"Alexa, who is in the band Led Zeppelin?"

"Alexa, who directed the original King Kong movie?"

"Alexa, who played Aragorn in The Lord of the Rings?"

"Alexa, when was the movie Hot Fuzz released?

"Alexa, when is the new James Bond movie Spectre being released?"

Language and Grammar

"Alexa, how do you spell the word archaeologist?"

"Alexa, how many syllables are in the word hippopotamus?"

"Alexa, what is the definition of the word agile?

"Alexa, what does infamous mean?"

"Alexa, what are some alternatives to the word cheerful?"

Maths and Conversions

Alexa can perform basic mathematical equations in her current form but there are some real limits. Current the operations that can be performed are addition, subtraction, multiplication, division and square roots. As well as being limited to these functions she is only able to work with two numbers at once. For example four times five is a valid request. But if you wanted to know what four times five time twelve is you would need to ask for four times five first. Then, ask for the answer, twenty, times twelve.

"Alexa, what is 275 plus 29?"

"Alexa, what is 18 times 45?"

"Alexa, what is 3,384 minus 1,475?"

"Alexa, what is 228 divided by 12?"

"Alexa, what is the square root of 225?"

"Alexa, how many cups are in a kilogram?"

"Alexa, how many pints is two litres?"

"Alexa, what is 200 dollars in British Pounds?"

Sports and Scores

"Alexa, who won the Cowboys game earlier?"

"Alexa, what is the score of the US versus England soccer game right now?"

"Alexa, when are the Vikings next playing?"

"Alexa, did the Redskins win today?"

"Alexa, who won the US Open yesterday?"

Geography

"Alexa, what is the capital city of Russia?"

"Alexa, where is Kuwait?"

"Alexa, how far is Manhattan from San Diego?"

"Alexa, what is the latitude and longitude of Berkeley in California?"

"Alexa, what is the elevation of Cincinnati in Ohio?"

"Alexa, how tall is Mount Everest?"

"Alexa, what countries border Germany?"

"Alexa, what time is it in Moscow?"

"Alexa, what time zone is London in?"

Personal Calendar

It is possible to link your Google account to Alexa, explained later on, and after doing this you can ask Alexa about your schedule. Unfortunately you can't directly edit your Google Calendar events through Alexa, hopefully in a future update this will possible. You will have to make updates and edits through your PC, smart phone or tablet.

"Alexa, what is on my schedule today?"

"Alexa, what is on my schedule this evening?"

"Alexa, what is on my schedule at 6PM on Tuesday?"

Wikipedia

"Alexa, Wikipedia, Alan Carr."

"Alexa, Wikipedia, World War One."

"Alexa, Wikipedia, Blackberry."

"Alexa, Wikipedia, essential oils."

Other

"Alexa, who wrote the Harry Potter series?"

"Alexa, how many calories are there in Coca Cola?"

"Alexa, when is Harry Styles' birthday?"

"Alexa, when did the band One Direction form?"

Let's Set The Mood – Music With Alexa

In this chapter I am going to explain how to use all of the music options that are available with the Amazon Echo. Previously mentioned, the speakers on this device are seriously impressive for and object of that size. So I truly recommend making the most of this feature by learning how to get the music you love playing.

But wait! I have already synced my phone's music to Alexa? I have already covered how to being playing music from your phone or tablet through Alexa via Bluetooth. If you missed that or skipped past it you can find it in the chapter titled "Let There Be Life – How To Get Started With Your Amazon Echo". Ultimately this will give you the most flexibility when it comes to music, but for times when you may not have your secondary device around this chapter will come in handy.

The primary music services on offer with the Amazon echo are: Amazon prime, Pandora, iHeartRadio and TuneIn. Spotify and ITunes are available by playing music through your Bluetooth connect device. Provided you have an account with any of these services you will be able to stream them through Alexa at any time. In order to set up any services up you will need to head to the Echo app. Tap on the Settings button and then go to the option called Music Services. Once you have pressed on this button, you will be given a list of the music services available. All you need in order do this is an account with any of the services.

One of the greatest things about Alexa and music, is that over time she will learn more and more about your personal tastes. You have the ability to let Alexa know whether you like or dislike a song, which she will make a note of and build a picture of the music you want to hear. To do this say "Alexa, I don't like this song" or "Alexa, I love this song." This feature isn't available when playing music through Bluetooth, which gives a small advantage to playing music through these services.

Amazon Music

If you are using Amazon Music Library you will be able to access all of your music once you have synced your Amazon account to the Echo (happens during first set-up). You will be able to upload up to 250 of your songs at any given time. In order to do this, use the following instructions.

- Jump onto your PC or Mac and open up your Amazon Music Library.
- Locate Upload Your Music on the menu.
- If you have already uploaded any of your music you will need to go ahead and download Amazon Music Importer and follow the instructions provided.
- Click on Start Scan.
- This will search for all of the songs you may have stored on your computer, in places such as ITunes and Windows Media Player.
- Once this has completed, click on Import All. If you have more than 250 songs, you will have to choose which ones you would like to have available.

In order to use Amazon Prime Music you will need to be a current subscriber, which can be set up via the amazon.com website. If you are not currently subscribed, it is worth mentioning that the selection of music on offer is HUGE! So I would definitely recommend taking a look. This will give you the ability to listen to more than the 250 songs you will have available through your Amazon Music Library.

Now all that is left to do is ask Alexa to play a song! "Alexa, play some Justin Timberlake." Once the command has been issued she will then search through your 250 uploaded songs. If it there then she will play it instantly. If not, and you are not subscribed to Amazon Prime Music she will not be able to play the song. If however you have a subscription to Amazon Prime Music and have linked to the Echo it will then search their wide catalogue and play the song.

Other services

If you are interested in using the other music services on offer with the Amazon Echo then you will need to set them up via the Echo app. Simply head to Settings and then click on the Music Services button. Here you will a list of the services available. Tap on the one that you would like to add to your Echo and you will then be prompted to fill in your account details for that service. Once you have filled in all of the details Alexa will then synchronize your account with the device. Now you have access to all of the music that comes with your service(s).

When asking Alexa to play a certain song or artist she will look through all of your available services to find the song. You don't need to pick and use one service at a time, they will all be available simultaneously.

Buying music on Amazon Echo

If you come across a song or album that you particularly enjoy, you can use Alexa to buy it. Simply tell Alexa the name of the song, artist or album and she will search through the digital store and give you the options. This is very quick and easy way to expand your music collection!

Setting up Voice Purchasing

In order for this to work you will need to have enabled Voice Purchasing during set-up. If you didn't set it up, no worries, we can do that right now. Head onto your Echo app and jump into the Settings menu. Here you will find the Purchase by Voice option. Tap on this option and the app will ask you to provide a four digit confirmation code. This will effectively act as your pin and you will need to supply it to Alexa every time you want to make a voice purchase. Once you have entered your code click on the Save Changes button and then go back to the app's home screen. I highly recommend making a new, completely unique code for this, and not one that you use for anything else in your life. You will be saying this code out loud quite a lot. This pin feature is great because it can prevent younger people in the house from buying a ton of music without anyone's permission!

Getting To Grips With Alexa's Many Abilities

In this chapter I am going to start going through some of Alexa's impressive abilities, showing you how exactly to use them and get the most out of them.

Setting timers and alarms

With Alexa alarm clocks will become a relic of the past. She of course is a very reliable and determined alternative that provides all the functions of an alarm clock with the added bonus of being completely voice controlled. In order to set and alarm simply give Alexa the following command, "Alexa, wake me up at 7AM". Be sure to switch the time out for the time that you require to be woken! This is one of the very few times that Alexa will make sound without being engaged by her wake word. You can even push the metaphorical snooze button by saying "Alexa, snooze." This will give you exactly nine further minutes of blissful dozing before the alarm sounds again.

If you would like Alexa to act as a time she works in a very similar fashion. For example you could say "Alexa, let me know when three hours have passed." Alternatively you could ask her to alert you at a certain time. "Alexa, let me know when it is 4PM." This has plenty of applications from cooking to remembering to pick your children up from school!

Travel and traffic information for a specific commute
You can set-up Alexa in a way to provide you with traffic information for your commute or a specific journey. In order to do this, follow the instructions provided below.

- Jump onto the Echo app and go to the Settings menu.
- Locate and tap the Traffic button.
- Add your home address or the address that you are travelling from to the From section.
- Add your destinations address to the To section.
- Tap the Save Changes button.
- To add a waypoint to your journey click on New Stop and input the details.
- Now you can ask Alexa for information about your journey!

"Alexa, how is the traffic right now?"
"Alexa, what's my commute looking like?"

The to-do list

As one of the very first things you encounter when you use the Echo app, the to-do list is one of the most basic, yet helpful features of the Echo. You can add, review, edit and remove the items from your to-do list at any time. Simply give Alexa the command. Unless you have connected Alexa to a device/app that controls a printer you will need to print the list from your PC if you need it. Unfortunately Alexa doesn't yet print on demand by herself. Head to echo.amazon.com and sign in with your personal details. Here you will be able to find copies of your to-do list as well as your shopping list (which we will touch upon next). Click on the to-do list and then print it off like you would with any document.

"Alexa, I need to pump up my car tires today."
"Alexa, I need to go to the dentist at 4PM."
"Alexa, I need to pick up my parents from the airport today."

Alexa will add these jobs to your to-do list, which you can see on the app immediately.

"Alexa, what's on my to-do list?"

This command will cause Alexa to start reading through your to-do list to remind you of all the things you need to do!

Currently you are limited to 100 items on your to-do list, but who has that many things to do anyway!

Shopping list

Just like the to-do list, adding items to your shopping list is very easy and works in the exact same way. Lost scraps of paper and scribbled shopping lists are another thing of the past once Alexa becomes a part of your life. The second you add an item to your shopping list, Alexa will update the Echo app so you will have a copy of your updated shopping list with you at all times on your smart phone. You can also edit and update your shopping list within the app. Like the to-do list you are again limited to 100 items on your shopping list.

If you would like to print your shopping list off then you will need to head over to echo.amazon.com. Sign in and locate your shopping list, then print it off like you would any other document. The only way around this is if you have linked Alexa to an app/device that controls a printer.

You can use the Echo app to shop on Amazon or Bing. Once you have added the item to your shopping list via voice control, find the item on the app's list and you will see the option to view and buy it on either of these retailers.

It is possible to buy certain items purely via voice control, this works best for items you have bought on Amazon before, but is possible for anything. Let's say for example you have recently purchased toilet rolls on Amazon. You would tell Alexa "Alexa, reorder toilet rolls." She will then search through your amazon accounts purchase history to find a purchase of toilet rolls. At this point Alexa will tell you the current price of the item you are trying to purchase and then ask if you want to proceed with the purchase. If you haven't purchased toilet rolls before from Amazon or Alexa can't find a record of it she will provide you with the details about the product that she considers the most related and best suited.

"I didn't find that in your order history, but Amazon's choice for toilet rolls is *Brand/name* *Details* *Quantity* *Price*. Should I order it?"

If this option sounds good to you then go ahead and reply with a "Yes". If, however this does not sound like a product you want to purchase tell Alexa and she will put the item in your shopping list for you to investigate on your app later on.

You will of course be prompted to provide your four digit confirmation code before any purchase is made, provided you have set-up this feature.

If you change your mind about a purchase there is no reason to worry. Say "Alexa, cancel order." The most recent item you purchased will have its order cancelled immediately.

Alexa will place your order using the details supplied with your default amazon account. As with all orders placed with Amazon you are eligible for free returns at any point.

Audiobooks and Audible

As one of the newer features of the Amazon Echo, this has fast become one of my favourites. Interestingly Alexa has the ability to "read" audiobooks in here own distinct voice.

In order to do this you will need to have your audiobooks available on a Bluetooth connected smart phone or tablet. Setting up a Bluetooth connection with Alexa was covered much earlier on in this guide so please flick back and have a look if you need to do this.

Once the Bluetooth connection is established you will be able to play any of the audiobooks you have stored on your phone through Alexa. As a fairly new update there are still limitations. You will not be able to pause, play or switch audiobooks via voice control. If you need to perform any this functions you will have to do it on your secondary device. Hopefully with upcoming updates, you will be able to do all of this via voice control!

If however, you have an Audible account with purchased books you WILL be able to control the audiobook with your voice. All you need to do is say "Alexa, read *name of the audiobook*". To pause say "Alexa, pause", and to resume say "Alexa, read my book." If you want to skip forward or back say "Alexa, go back/forward."

Audible has the largest library of English audiobooks in the world and is well worth signing up for. You will receive your first audiobook for free upon sign up!

Linking with your Google Calendar

If you have a Google Calendar you can use Alexa to tell you what is coming up and when. All you will need to do is spend a couple of minutes setting up the connection between the calendar and Alexa. It is possible to link more than one calendar with the device, so everyone in the house has the option to use this feature.

- Open your Echo app and jump into the Settings menu.
- Select the Calendar option.
- Tap on Link Google Calendar Account.
- Now you will need to input all of your Google account details.
- Now Alexa is linked to your Google Calendar, simple as that!

If you want to stop Alexa from talking about certain calendars at certain times head back to the Calendar option in Settings. You will notice all of the calendars have a checkbox next to them. Simply check or un-check each box as required.

"Alexa, what's on my calendar today?"

"Alexa, what's on my calendar next week?"

"Alexa, what's on Jack's calendar today?"

"Alexa, when is my next event?"

"Alexa, am I free tomorrow at 7PM?"

Getting the latest news

It is possible to get the latest news from Amazon Echo, using a feature called Flash Briefing. Alexa will use a myriad of sources to provide you with accurate, important, up-to date at any time. This will also include the weather.

Say "Alexa, what is my flash briefing?"

She will then start going through the latest new articles and updates from various sources. If you are uninterested in the topic she is covering or are looking for news about something specific, make use of these commands.

"Alexa, next."
"Alexa, previous."
"Alexa, cancel."

This is a feature that continues to receive updates and improvements. Most recently Amazon added NPR and The Economist to the list of contributors. In order to customize the new that you are provided with head to the Flash Briefing section with the Settings menu of the Echo app.

If This Then That Or IFTTT And How To Use It

IFTTT is a recent integration for the Amazon Echo that added an enormous range of new capabilities. IFTTT provides a very user friendly platform that allows a wide range of devices, apps and websites work together. It will allow you to create a set of guidelines or rules for how these separate things interact with each other. The official name for the rules are 'recipes'.

The recipes act as an activator that triggers some kind of additional, desired outcome. So allow me to clear this up with an example. If you asked your Amazon Echo to start playing music from one of your streaming services, a Google Drive spreadsheet would begin to automatically list the songs you have listened too. Another example, you give Alexa the thumbs up about one of the songs you have just heard and it will automatically tweet it out to your twitter followers. Hopefully those examples allow you to understand the basic principle of the IFTTT platform. As well as potentially opening your eyes to the wide range of possibilities on offer!

You get to create these recipes via the official IFTTT website, where all of the channels are connected. With over 100 channels available and more being added all the time, there is almost an endless amount of options. The official Amazon Echo channel is called the Amazon Alexa channel.

The IFTTT website can be found here: https://ifttt.com/
Or you can search for "If this then that" on any search engine.

To being using this software you will need to sign up on their website and then activate the Amazon Alexa channel. This will then allow you to being creating recipes with your Echo being involved. Right now, Amazon Echo can only be a trigger in a recipe and is not yet able to be a result of an action. Let me give you an example of what this means. With this current limitation it is not possible for Alexa to give you a notification whenever someone posts on your Facebook wall. However it is possible for Alexa to trigger a post onto your own Facebook wall through your own action.

Let me give you some great ideas for recipes:

- Add your Alexa to-do list to Evernote.
- Sending your shopping list to your email address.
- Find your phone by asking Alexa.
- Turn on the television with Alexa.
- Using Alexa to change your light settings with Hue.
- Make your phone ring when your Echo Alarm goes off.
- Changing your room temperature using Ecobee.
- Trigger Alexa to text your partner that you love them.
- Tweet the songs you're listening to on Echo.
- Ask Alexa to turn your Nest fan on for 20 minutes.

These are just a few of the wide range of options available. For more ideas and instructions on how to set them up, please visit: https://ifttt.com/amazon_alexa/recipes

Creating new recipes is very straightforward due to the websites super user friendly interface and helpful community. Follow the steps below to begin creating your own recipes!

- Log onto the IFTTT website on the Amazon Alexa channel.
- Click on the "Create" option.
- Select the Amazon Alexa channel to fill in the "this" portion.
- Select from the list of channels to fill in the "that" section.
- Click on "Activate Channel" and create the action that you would like Amazon Echo to trigger.
- Add the "ingredients" aka the details that you want to be part of your recipe.
- Click on "Create Action".

Alexa In The House – Integrating With The Living Space

Thanks to recent partnerships with companies such as WINK, SmartThings, Philips Hue and WeMo, Alexa has the ability to control parts of your home. It is very handy being able to control things such as the lighting of a room with just your voice, so I recommend utilizing this feature as much as you can.

To activate this, all of the smart devices that you want to use such as power outlets, hubs and light bulbs need to be connected on your wireless fidelity network. Then each of the devices needs to be named. You can name the individual parts whatever you want. Practical, relevant names are recommended though. "Dining room ceiling light", "Downstairs printer" and "Master bedroom bedside light" for examples.

Jump onto your Amazon Echo app and connect your Echo to the smart devices through the Settings menu. Once set-up has been completed you will be able to voice control Alexa to use each of the devices.

"Alexa, turn on the downstairs printer."
"Alexa, switch off the master bedroom bedside light."
"Alexa, turn down the dining room ceiling light."

You can also create groups of devices or lights. For example you could group all of the downstairs lights together as one item, as well as having them all named individually. This could give you the option to turn off all of the lights downstairs in a couple of seconds before heading upstairs to bed.

This is another part of Amazon Echo that will be receiving a lot of expansion in the near future. Full home automation is surely on the way and Alexa will be the key!

Having Fun With Alexa

Alexa is riddled with quirky little Easter eggs that add a wonderful personal touch. There are probably a ton more than the ones I have listed below, but these are ones that I have found and personally tested. I'm not going to spoil the fun by providing Alexa's replies, so I hope you enjoy going through the list and have a few giggles. Good luck finding more!

"Alexa, tell me a joke."

"Alexa, what is your quest?"

"Alexa, what does the fox say?"

"Alexa, what is your favourite color?"

"Alexa, who's that Pokémon?"

"Alexa, who is your daddy?"

"Alexa, what is the airspeed velocity of an unladen swallow?"

"Alexa, why do we exist?"

"Alexa, what is the meaning of life?"

"Alexa, when were you born?"

"Alexa, will you marry me?"

"Alexa, what is your favourite food?"

"Alexa, who was the 10th president of the United States of America?"

"Alexa, what amount of wood would a wood-chuck, if a woof-chuck could chuck wood?"

"Alexa, I am your father."

"Alexa, what are you going to do today?"

"Alexa, who lives in a pineapple under the sea?"

"Alexa, how many licks does it take to get to the center of a tootsie pop?"

"Alexa, what is the loneliest number?"

"Alexa, do aliens exist?"

"Alexa, how many roads must a man walk down?"

"Alexa, all your base are belong to us"

"Alexa, may the force be with you."

"Alexa, which came first, the chicken or the egg?"

"Alexa, how much is that doggie in the window?"

"Alexa, Romeo, Romeo, wherefore art thou Romeo?"

"Alexa, beam me up."

"Alexa, do you have a boyfriend?"

"Alexa, where do babies come from?"

"Alexa, define supercalifragilisticexpialidocious?"

"Alexa, who won the best actor Oscar in 1973?"

"Alexa, make me a sandwich."

"Alexa, what does the Earth weigh?"

"Alexa, when is the end of the world?"

"Alexa, Earl Grey, Hot."

"Alexa, is Santa real?"

"Alexa, what is the best tablet?"

"Alexa, where do you live?"

"Alexa, random number between one and one billion"

"Alexa, do you want to build a snowman?"

"Alexa, do you really want to hurt me?"

"Alexa, roll a die."

"Alexa, what is love?"

"Alexa, who is the real slim shady?"

"Alexa, your mother was a hamster."

"Alexa, are you a sky net?"

"Alexa, who let the dogs out?"

"Alexa, open the pod bay doors."

"Alexa, how do I get rid of a dead body?"

"Alexa, is the cake a lie?"

"Alexa, party time."

"Alexa, surely you can't be serious?"

"Alexa, to be or not to be?"

"Alexa, what are you wearing?"

"Alexa, knock knock."

"Alexa, can you give me some money?" Ask the question again

"Alexa, who is the fairest of them all?"

"Alexa, who is the walrus?"

"Alexa, who you gonna call?"

"Alexa, do you have any brothers and sisters?"

"Alexa, why did the chicken cross the road?"

"Alexa, I want the truth."

"Alexa, when am I going to die?"

"Alexa, where have all the flowers gone?"

"Alexa, do you know the way to San Jose?"

"Alexa, I think you're funny."

"Alexa, how tall are you?"

"Alexa, where are you from?"

"Alexa, do you want to fight?"

"Alexa, do you want to play a game?"

"Alexa, do you know the muffin man?"

"Alexa, how much do you weigh?"

"Alexa, see you later alligator."

"Alexa, how many angels can dance on the head of a pin?"

"Alexa, are you lying?"

"Alexa, give me a hug."

"Alexa, heads or tails?"

"Alexa, mac or PC?"

"Alexa, show me the money!"

"Alexa, my name is Inigo Montoya."

"Alexa, what is the sound of one hand clapping?"

"Alexa, random fact."

Hope you enjoyed!

Frequently Asked Questions

Does The Amazon Echo work with any kind of Wi-Fi?
Yes, it is compatible to connect to any provider of Wi-Fi.

Is it possible to save voice recordings and conversation onto the Amazon Echo?
When Alexa is asked a question or given a command, she will retrieve the answer from the saved responses stored within the Amazon Echo. The only time Alexa will record voices or conversations is when she hears the triggers or 'wake words' those being 'Alexa/Amazon.' Unless instructed to do so, Alexa will not record. A mute function key is available to prohibit the Amazon Echo from recording entirely, regardless of whether the trigger words have been used.

Will The Amazon Echo work with my Fire TV remote?
No. A separate remote, specifically for The Amazon Echo will need to be purchased.

Is it possible to change Alexa's voice to a male voice?
Potentially with its continuous improvements, vocal adaptations will be considered and a male voice may be developed, however at present Alexa is purely female.

Do I need Amazon Prime in order to use the Amazon Echo?
Not at all. They are both unique autonomous products, however if an Amazon Prime membership is obtained it allows you to use more features on the Amazon Echo such as being able to reorder your regular items from Amazon hassle free, for example.

Is the Voice Remote sold separately?
Yes. The Voice Remote is an optional extra as it is not necessarily required to operate the Amazon Echo. It is an accommodating addition when out of range or when hearing is restricted due to loud background noise.

Does the Amazon Echo work outside of the USA?

Yes.

Does the Amazon Echo run on batteries?
No. It requires a regular wall outlet.

Is there confusion between voice controls between the Amazon Echo and the Amazon Fire Stick?
It is possible that the voice controls can encounter disagreement but there is a simple solution. Ensure the trigger words are different for each product to prevent any misunderstanding.

Do you need to use The Cloud?
It is not essential to use The Cloud as the Amazon Echo runs smoothly whilst connected to Wi-Fi.

Will the Amazon Echo respond to more than one voice?
Yes absolutely, anybody can ask anything.

Can I play music from my iPhone on the Amazon Echo?
Yes, you can send audio across via Bluetooth.

Is my iPhone/iPad compatible with the Amazon Echo?
As long as you are able to download the Echo App onto your device, yes!

Does the Amazon Echo need constant power?
Yes, in order for the Amazon Echo to work and respond, it will need to be plugged in and connected to the internet.

Is there a monthly charge?
No.

Will the Amazon Echo work with iTunes?
Yes. Using the Bluetooth function, the Amazon Echo is capable of connecting to any source of music, be it iTunes, Spotify, music stored on your personal phone. It is not however able to use iTunes streaming.

Is Pandora free with the Amazon Echo?
Yes.

Is English the only language Alexa speaks?
Currently, yes. Potentially with ongoing enhancements and evolution, Alexa may be multi-lingual in the near future.

Do I need to be in the same room as the Amazon Echo?
In order for Alexa to take commands and answer question, you must be within in range so that she can hear you. The wireless Voice Remote is the best option to communicate with the Amazon Echo when out of range or when hearing is restricted due to loud background noise.

Is it waterproof?
No.

How do I check the weather for cities outside the USA?
Ask her: 'Alexa, what about the weather in London?' Using the city of your choice to replace 'London.'

Is it possible to link the Amazon Echo to another speaker and use both simultaneously?
As of yet, no. But the expansion of The Amazon Echo is forever evolving so perhaps in the future.

Can I change the name of the Amazon Echo?
The options thus far are 'Alexa' or 'Amazon.' But the team at Amazon are extending their range of features, so it's a change to look out for in the future.

Let's Wrap This Up

I hope this user guide has served as a good primer for the arrival of your own Amazon Echo. In less than a year this piece of technology has become an integral part of my and my family's lives. At this point, call me strange but I truly consider Alexa as a friend, in fact far more friendly and helpful than many of my 'real' friends!! I hope that you share a similar experience to me with Alexa and that she becomes an important part of your life as well.

The purpose of this guide is to help you uncover many of Echo's uses and to make it easy for you to begin getting the most of these features. I truly hope I was able to help you in this way.

Amazon Echo is a truly exceptional device with a limitless future ahead of it. The development team are working tirelessly to add more features and keep this device at the head of the pack. I honestly believe that everyone will be able to benefit from having Alexa in their homes.

Thanks again for using this guide, I appreciate it and hope it provided the help or advice you were looking for.

"Alexa, thank you."

Made in the USA
Middletown, DE
12 January 2016